1 5 0
Opening and Closing
P R A Y E R S

D0089649

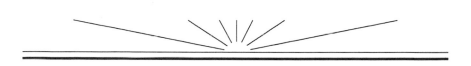

1 5 0
Opening and Closing
PRAYERS

by
CARL KOCH

Saint Mary's Press
Christian Brothers Publications
Winona, Minnesota

To Susan and Lanny Harmon,
God's blessings of peace and love!

Genuine recycled paper with 10% post-consumer waste.
Printed with soy-based ink.

The publishing team included Robert P. Stamschror, development editor; Mary Duerson, copy editor; Gary J. Boisvert, production editor and typesetter; and Evy Abrahamson, cover designer and illustrator; and pre-press, printing, and binding by the graphics division of Saint Mary's Press.

The psalms quoted in this book are from *Psalms Anew: In Inclusive Language,* by Nancy Shreck, OSF, and Maureen Leach, OSF. Copyright © 1986 by Saint Mary's Press.

Some of the scriptural material on pages 15, 17, 19, 51, 59, 67, 70, and 71 is adapted to make the text inclusive regarding gender. These adaptations are not to be understood or used as official translations of the Bible. All other scriptural quotations used in this book are from the New Jerusalem Bible. Copyright © 1985 by Darton, Longman and Todd, Ltd., and Doubleday, a division of Bantam, Doubleday, Dell Publishing Group, Inc. Reprinted by permission of the publisher.

Printed in the United States of America

Printing: 11 10 9

Year: 2001 00

ISBN 0-88489-241-7

Contents

Introduction

150 Opening and Closing Prayers will be helpful to anyone who wants to begin or end a meeting, a school day, or a class with a prayer but does not always have time to compose one. The prayers in this book cover many themes in Christian life, and each prayer may be adapted to varying situations.

One important feature of the prayers is that they each employ a passage from either the Hebrew Scriptures or the Christian Testament. By using scriptural passages, the prayers not only lift the attention of those praying to God but also proclaim God's word. The prayers communicate to God and provide a way for those praying to listen to what God has to say.

Using These Prayers

At the beginning of each unit of prayers, three opening statements are offered. These statements call those praying into God's presence. Three types of statements for the call to presence are offered:
1. *proclamations* that announce God's presence
2. *petitions* that assume God's presence
3. *invitations* that ask the people to place themselves in God's presence

Select the opening statement that best fits the prayer you have chosen and the circumstances in which you are praying. Pausing briefly after this opening statement allows for recollection or calming before the prayer proper.

Read each prayer slowly and naturally. Permit the words to sink in. If a pause is indicated, take it.

Practicing the prayers beforehand will enhance their effectiveness. The prayers combine four modes:
- scriptural passages
- reflections
- responsorials
- invitations

Being aware of these different modes of prayer and distinguishing them by way of pauses and voice inflections will make the prayers more meaningful and evocative. Practicing the prayers becomes more important if they are to be read over a public address system.

After you have read a prayer, you may wish to add a short prayer of your own that personalizes it for the community. For instance, after a prayer of praise and thanksgiving, you might say something like, "Tonight, we thank God especially for . . ."

In many of the prayers, the last line serves as a good ending, but a distinct closing line is also provided for each unit of prayers. So to end a prayer, just use the final line, use the ending line as given at the end of each prayer theme, or create one of your own.

Finally, although most people will use the prayers for opening and closing various gatherings or at the start or finish of a school day, you may also use the prayers as
- morning or evening prayers
- meal prayers
- parts of longer prayer services
- sources of reflection or meditation
- prayers for any occasion

Hopefully, however you use the prayers, they will help you and your community communicate with God and listen to God's word.

CHAPTER 1

Celebration and Thanksgiving

Call to presence

- Let us remember that our bountiful God is with us today in this place.
- The God who gives us all things is present.
- Gracious God, here present, listen as we pray.

Prayers

Psalm 139:13–14

Psalm 139 declares:

> [God,] You created my inmost being
> and knit me together in my mother's womb.
> For all these mysteries—
> for the wonder of myself,
> for the wonder of your works—
> I thank you.

We do thank you, God, for the wonder of ourselves, because we are unique, marvelous, talented creations of your hands.

May we appreciate and value all the wonder of our life and the wonders of people and nature. In valuing people and nature, may we protect, affirm, and build a better, more peaceful world.

John 10:10

Jesus tells us,

> I have come
> so that they may have life
> and have it to the full.

Jesus wants us to enjoy the many great things in life. For a moment, let's remember some of the truly good things God has given us that make life enjoyable and fulfilling. [Pause briefly.]

Thank you, God, for all these gifts that make our life full. Thank you especially for Jesus' coming to live with us. He showed us how to love.

James 1:16–17

Today, let us give thanks for all the wonders around us, remembering what James said in his letter, "Make no mistake about this . . . : all that is good, all that is perfect, is given us from above."

So thank you, God, for our friends, our family, and all those who share their goodness with us. Thank you for nature with its many wonders—the seasons, the rain for the crops and flowers, doves and eagles, rabbits and foxes, all living things. Thank you for kind works, for praise, for our talents, for our skills, for learning and teaching, for hope in the future. For all things, we thank you.

Each of us, in silence, can offer thanks in our own way. [Pause.]

1 Peter 4:9

Our God is revealed as a God of open arms who always welcomes us with care and protection. Saint Peter says, "Welcome each other into your houses without grumbling."

The feeling of welcome is a good one, and it comes not only when we are welcomed into a house but also when we are welcomed into a conversation, into a group activity, into another person's joys and fears.

Thank you, God, for those who have opened their home, mind, and heart to us.

May we do likewise.

Colossians 1:3–4

As the Apostle Paul says, "We give thanks for you to God . . . continually in our prayers, ever since we heard about your faith in Christ Jesus and the love that you show towards all God's holy people."

Thank you, God, for those who love us—those who are there when we need encouragement, a kindly ear, a good talking to, a pat on the back, a shared meal, or the gift of their time. Thank you, God, for our ability to show love to other people, for the times when we have encouraged, listened, shared advice, patted another's back, shared a meal, or given our time. For all these gifts of love, we give you thanks.

Psalm 118:1

Psalm 118 begins by saying:

Alleluia!
I give thanks to you, Yahweh, for you are good;
your love is everlasting!

God gives us unconditional, totally faithful love. As humans we usually condition our love, and we are not always faithful. But let us thank God for our friends and those people who love us and are loyal in their support and affection for us. They are good. They are precious gifts from a loving God.

So we thank God for them, and maybe today we can thank each of our friends for being our friends.

James 1:19

We like to be listened to; it makes us feel as if we are taken seriously and valued. For this reason James remarks in his epistle, "Remember this . . . : everyone should be quick to listen but slow to speak and slow to human anger."

Listening is a great gift that you, God, and the people in our life can give us.

For all those who have heard us out, who let us share our pain and joy, who have taken our words and feelings seriously, who have valued and appreciated what we have said—for all our listener friends, we give you thanks, God who always listens.

May we listen for others too.

Matthew 5:16

In Matthew's Gospel, Jesus says, "'Your light must shine in people's sight, so that, seeing your good works, they may give praise'" to God.

For a moment, let us silently recall some of the good that we have done for other people. [Pause.]

Now let us celebrate these good works and thank God for giving us the grace to do them.

Thank you, God, for the goodness that resides within us. Nourish our ability to do good. Thank you, all-good God.

Matthew 9:12–13

God sent Jesus to heal our wounds, teach us wisdom, and show us mercy. His words and works manifest God's gracious love for us. In Matthew's Gospel, Jesus proclaims: "'It is not the healthy who need the doctor, but the sick. . . . I came to call not the upright, but sinners.'"

No doubt exists about the fact that we are sinners. You call us, Jesus. You heal us.

For our wholeness and health of spirit, we thank you and celebrate.

Matthew 26:28

God sent Jesus to lift us out of hopelessness and sin and to teach us charity and peace.

Matthew's Gospel tells us that at the Last Supper, Jesus gave us his body and blood "'poured out for many for the forgiveness of sins.'"

With joyous celebration we give you thanks and praise for this perfect gift of Jesus. We have new and full life with him. His blood has washed our souls; his body nourishes us to eternal life. Blessed and holy, gracious and good are you, our saving God.

Romans 5:2

We rejoice in our salvation by Jesus the Christ. Saint Paul writes, "It is through him, by faith, that we have been admitted into God's favour in which we are living, and look forward exultantly to God's glory."

All praise and thanks are yours, Jesus our Savior. You have set us free from sin. We hope in glory because we live in God's favor.

May we always praise you and celebrate our salvation by good works and acts of peace.

Romans 8:14–17

Through Jesus we have become children of God. So Saint Paul says: "All who are guided by the Spirit of God are sons [and daughters] of God. . . . And if we are children, then we are heirs, heirs of God and joint-heirs with Christ."

Our inheritance is not gold or jewels, mansions or fast cars. Our inheritance is a life liberated from the darkness of self-centeredness and purposelessness. We are children of light and love learned from Jesus.

All praise and glory are yours, our gracious God. We are your children. May we play before you, laughing and full.

John 3:17

John's Gospel proclaims that God sent Jesus

"into the world
not to judge the world,
but so that through him the world might be saved."

We celebrate the always-present Spirit of Jesus in our heart and in all your creation. That you would send your own child to set us free from sin and death is a fact we cannot completely understand. But we can and do thank you, praise you, and celebrate the wonder of your love for us.

May we always be mindful of your awesome gift.

John 12:46

In John's Gospel, John tells us that Jesus came

> "into the world as light,
> to prevent anyone who believes . . .
> from staying in the dark any more."

The faith, hope, and love you taught and modeled are a bright flame in the darkness. Your light guides us to fullness of days. Glory is your name, our light. The heat from your light warms our heart.

May we remember your light today when we see the radiant sun, a burning candle, or a shining lamp. Jesus, our light, we praise and thank you. Shine on us forever.

John 14:16–18

We celebrate God's presence in the Spirit sent to be with us when Jesus rose, and with us ever since. As Jesus said,

> "I shall ask the Father,
> and he will give you another Paraclete
> to be with you for ever,
> the Spirit of truth . . .
> you know him,
> because he is with you, he is in you.
> I shall not leave you orphans."

You, Spirit, are in and with us now and always. Even if we sometimes forget your presence, you call us back and remind us that you are here. Your presence is light and warmth to our soul, and so we celebrate and thank you.

May we always take notice of your holy dwelling place within. We are not orphans and never will be.

Acts 2:12–13

The Spirit of the living God inflamed the disciples on Pentecost. The Scriptures tell us that the crowd that gathered to listen to them "was amazed and perplexed; they asked one another what it all meant. Some, however, laughed it off. 'They have been drinking too much new wine,' they said."

When we are on fire with your Spirit, we are intoxicated by the warmth of your love flowing in us. Such love is "new wine" because we cannot feel it from any other source.

Fill us now with this new wine of your Spirit. We praise and thank you for your wondrous gift. We celebrate the fire of your love.

2 Corinthians 9:10–11

Saint Paul reminds us, "The one who so freely provides seed for the sower and food to eat will provide you with ample store . . . : you will be rich enough in every way for every kind of generosity that makes people thank God."

Generous God, you have given amply to people who have given generously to us. In the silence of our heart, we now lift up the names of those who have given us their time, talents, and other gifts. [Pause.]

Thank you, God, for all these people. Bless and hold them in the palm of your hand.

Adapted from Ephesians 1:3–6

Blessed be you, God, for you have blessed us with all the spiritual gifts through Christ. You have chosen us in Christ, even before the Creation, to be holy and blameless before you in love, picking us out for yourself to be your adopted children through Jesus. This was your will and good pleasure. All praise and celebration to you, God of mercy.

Adapted from Colossians 1:3

Let us give thanks for the love we have been shown.

First, let's offer thanks to God for members of our family who have nourished and loved us. [Pause.] We give thanks to God for them.

Next, let's offer thanks to God for friends who support and encourage us. [Pause.] We give thanks to God for them.

May grace and peace be always with those who love us and those we love.

Ending

All praise and thanks to you, our God, source of all that is good. Amen. Alleluia!

CHAPTER 2

Compassion and Service

Call to presence

- Let us remember that the God of mercy is with us now.

- A kind and compassionate God is in our midst, as we pray.

- All-good God, may we rest in your compassionate presence here.

Prayers

John 8:7

Jesus confounded the crowd of people who were ready to stone the woman caught committing adultery. Instead of picking up a stone to join in the execution demanded by the Law, he looked the people square in the eyes and challenged them: "'Let the one among you who is guiltless be the first to throw a stone at her.'"

Jesus, you challenge us with these same words because all too often we are ready to throw stones at people who offend us, who look different, or who do not measure up to our high standards.

Jesus, may we remember your compassion and justice today. Help us to straighten out our own faults before we mess around with other people's lives. You know that we have plenty of quirks and problems ourselves.

Adapted from Mark 9:41 _____

One day Jesus told a group of people, "If people give you a cup of water to drink because you belong to Christ, then in truth I tell you, they will most certainly not lose their reward."

Overlooking the little acts of kindness that we do is easy, but Jesus knew that these little acts are important.

With God's help, may we share the cup of kindness with our sisters and brothers today. May the people with whom we come into contact leave our company refreshed. And may God help us to serve people who need food, water, shelter, and clothing.

Adapted from 1 John 3:17 _____

Saint John told his friends,

> If people are well off in worldly possessions
> and see their neighbors in need
> but close their hearts to them,
> how can the love of God be remaining in them?

Jesus, you who healed the sick, fed the hungry, and spoke words of hope, grant us the grace to give generously from what we have, whether of our money, time, talents, joy, or hope.

You give us all that we have and intend that we share with our sisters and brothers. Teach us generosity and openness of heart and action.

Matthew 25:45 _____

Jesus always took special care of hungry, poor, thirsty, homeless, and imprisoned people. Our salvation is determined by how we treat them. He warns us, "'So far as you neglected to do this to one of the least of these, you neglected to do it to me.'"

By identifying yourself with prisoners, homeless folk, victims of hunger and thirst, you made clear the path to you. That path will take us on a search for justice, to soup kitchens and shelters, to prisons and the streets.

Give us the grace of charity. Help us see you, Jesus, in all people, especially in your poor people.

Colossians 3:12

The Apostle Paul reminds us that God's love makes us special. He says, "As the chosen of God, then, the holy people whom [God] loves, you are to be clothed in heartfelt compassion, in generosity and humility, gentleness and patience."

God had so much compassion that God sent Jesus to us, and Jesus shows us how to be humble, gentle, and patient.

Loving God, help us to follow the model of your Son as we get on with our life today.

Romans 12:13

Saint Paul reminds us to "share with any of God's holy people who are in need; look for opportunities to be hospitable."

May we share and be hospitable. In this way we make friends with new people and with Jesus the Christ and our Brother.

John 13:12–15

At the Last Supper, Jesus washed the feet of the Apostles. Then he said, "'Do you understand . . . what I have done to you? . . . If I, then, the Lord and Master, have washed your feet, you must wash each other's feet. I have given you an example so that you may copy what I have done to you.'"

Jesus, you made compassionate service a central part of the lifestyle of Christians. You showed us how to be hospitable, caring, and generous, how to build community.

May we follow your example today.

Matthew 5:4

Jesus tells us that "blessed are the gentle: / they shall have the earth as inheritance."

It's not always easy to be gentle. We're told to be tough, competitive, and assertive. But there are times when we like to be soothed and treated gently. We treat packages with gentleness when they are labeled, "fragile, handle with care."

So, compassionate God, give us the sensitivity and courage to be gentle with other people. Help us to hear the anguish and hurt in others' lives and to treat them with the kindly care of Jesus.

James 2:13 _____

Jesus taught us how to be merciful. He healed the sick, opened the eyes of the blind, and even forgave those who crucified him. James says, "Whoever acts without mercy will be judged without mercy but mercy can afford to laugh at judgement."

Merciful Jesus, once again remind us about how to be merciful. We desire mercy for ourselves; may we be merciful to other people—people who are weaker than us, or poorer, or less clever or athletic, less attractive or less able. Perhaps if we are merciful to other people, we will receive mercy when we need it.

Thank you, Jesus of mercy, for your compassion to us.

Matthew 5:7 _____

One of the Beatitudes is "blessed are the merciful: / they shall have mercy shown them."

We can all remember instances when we needed a little mercy. Maybe we needed an extension on a project. Maybe we needed a loan. Or, as is often the case, we needed forgiveness from someone whom we had hurt. Remember the sigh of relief when mercy was granted and the grief and disappointment when mercy was denied.

All merciful God, you give us what we need and constantly forgive us. Now, grant us the will to be generous in mercy toward our sisters and brothers. May we be people of mercy and forgiveness.

Adapted from 2 Corinthians 9:6–7 _____

Saint Paul says: Remember—anyone who sows sparsely will reap sparsely as well—and anyone who sows generously will reap generously as well. People should give as much as they have decided on their own initiative, not reluctantly or under compulsion, for God loves a cheerful giver.

Cheerful giving is a goal worth praying for and working toward, but there is just enough selfishness in most of us that taints the joy of compassion.

Create a generous spirit in us, all-good God. May we sow generously and happily, and reap the same way.

Ending

We offer this prayer in the name of Jesus, the source of all compassion. Amen.

CHAPTER 3

Courage in Hard Times

Call to presence

- All-powerful God, you dwell within us. Hear our prayer.

- The gracious God is with us in our weakness and our strength, as we pray.

- Let us recall that the God of the universe resides in our midst.

Prayers

John 18:25

We might become discouraged by not standing up for the Christian values we profess, by doing what we don't want to do, by our slipshod commitment to justice, honesty, peacefulness, and charity. As we pray today, let us remember Peter, first among the Apostles, beloved by Jesus. When asked by someone, "'Aren't you another of his disciples?' He denied it saying, 'I am not.'"

In this instance, Peter lacked courage too, but later, with God's help, he stood in front of anyone who would hear and proclaimed the word of God, knowing full well that he was putting his life on the line.

God, grant us courage to live justly, love bravely, and be people of peace. Support us in our failings because we will need your generous forgiveness.

James 1:13–14

Saint James was inspired to give his followers some tough advice. He said: "Never, when you are being put to the test, say, 'God is tempting me'; . . . [God] does not put anybody to the test. Everyone is put to the test by being attracted and seduced by that person's own wrong desire."

Merciful God, it is easy for us to blame you when things go wrong and when we do bad things. Our own Christian adulthood means that we accept the full weight of our actions.

Help us to be honest with ourselves and courageously face the challenge to live just and honest lives.

John 15:16–17

We have been chosen by Jesus. He has saved us and taught us how to love. Jesus said,

> You did not choose me,
> no, I chose you;
> and I commissioned you
> to go out and to bear fruit. . . .
> My command to you
> is to love one another.

Being chosen by our God makes us special, but being special comes with the responsibility to bear fruit through our charity or love. Love demands courage.

God, give us courage to care, to love. Sharpen our resolve; sensitize our spirits; strengthen our heart.

Romans 7:21–23

Paul describes our situation when he says, "I find this rule: that for me, where I want to do nothing but good, evil is close at my side. In my inmost self I dearly love God's law, but I see that acting on my body there is a different law which battles against the law in my mind."

Jesus, blessed friend, conflict afflicts us constantly. We want to do the right thing, the just thing, the loving thing, but we turn aside from what we intend. Jesus, this stress and guilt turns to opportunity only if we turn to you, the one source of hope, the one source of freedom.

Be at our side today, Jesus. May we do the good that we intend and avoid the destructiveness of which we are capable.

Romans 8:26–27 _____

In times of weakness, the Holy Spirit gives us courage. Saint Paul says: "The Spirit too comes to help us in our weakness, for, when we do not know how to pray properly, then the Spirit personally makes our petitions for us . . . ; the prayers that the Spirit makes for God's holy people are always in accordance with the mind of God."

We invite you, Spirit of truth, into our inmost being. Be with us in our times of testing and when we need courage, especially during times when we are tempted to be destructive, bitter, or passive in the face of injustice.

Come, Holy Spirit, give us courage.

Matthew 5:44 _____

Jesus says, "'Love your enemies and pray for those who persecute you.'"

Jesus, these are hard words. They demand more than we are capable of. Loving our friends and family is hard enough, but our enemies—it seems impossible. Only you can give us the courage to forgive our enemies, respect them, and do justice to them.

Please, Jesus, send us strength to care for our enemies. With your aid all things are possible, even this.

Romans 5:3–5 _____

Hardships are opportunities for growth in new life. Saint Paul tells us: "Let us exult, too, in our hardships, understanding that hardship develops perseverance, and perseverance develops a tested character, something that gives us hope, and a hope which will not let us down, because the love of God has been poured into our hearts by the Holy Spirit which has been given to us."

Spirit of God, help us to persevere in our hardships, so that we become more like Jesus the Christ, the man for others.

Rather than despair, may we put on hope.

Ending

Hear our prayer, God our rock of strength and courage. Amen.

CHAPTER 4

Creating Community

Call to presence

- The God of unity is present with us as we pray.

- Let us remember that when we gather in God's name, God is in our midst.

- God with us, make us one in mind and heart, as we pray.

Prayers

Proverbs 11:2 _____

Proverbs says: "Pride comes first; disgrace soon follows; / with the humble is wisdom found."

Creator God, help us today to listen to one another and appreciate what each one has to offer, so that by day's end we will be just a bit wiser and avoid the disgrace that comes from pride.

Proverbs 10:18 _____

The loving God tells us in Proverbs: "Liars' lips are a cover for hatred, / whoever utters slander is a fool."

It is easy to fall into the foolishness of bad-mouthing other people and to be careless with the truth. Most of us want to be positive about other people, so guide our tongue today.

Maybe if we speak truth and give affirmation to others, we will feel better about ourselves and your world.

Mark 4:33 _____

In the words of Saint Mark's Gospel, Jesus "spoke the word to them, so far as they were capable of understanding it."

Jesus, you communicated with people at their level of ability. Today, as we talk with other people, help us to speak plainly and clearly, realizing that most people want to understand us.

Guide our efforts to be honest and open with other people, not expecting that everyone will comprehend our meaning right away. Grant us patience and persistence in our attempts to understand one another.

2 Corinthians 8:13–14 _____

Just God, help us to create community among our friends, in our neighborhoods and schools, in our country, and in the world.

Your disciple Paul tells us where to start, by sharing with people in need. "It is not that you ought to relieve other people's needs and leave yourselves in hardship," he says. "But there should be a fair balance—your surplus at present may fill their deficit, and another time their surplus may fill your deficit. So there may be a fair balance."

May we be generous enough to seek a fair balance in the necessities of life, so that we build up the whole community of humankind. On this planet, we ultimately survive or perish together. Just God, guide us to a fair balance.

Matthew 15:18–19 _____

Jesus, you say, "'Whatever comes out of the mouth comes from the heart, and it is this that makes someone unclean. For from the heart come evil intentions.'"

Cleanse our heart of evil intentions as we gather together today. Give us hearts to do good.

Instead of injury, may our heart be filled with kind words. Instead of slander, may we be gently honest. Instead of theft or cheating, may we be generous with what we have. Jesus, cleanse our heart of evil intentions.

Acts 2:44–47 _____

Christ calls us to build community as described in the Acts of the Apostles: "All who shared the faith owned everything in common; they sold their goods and possessions and distributed the proceeds among themselves according to what each one needed. . . . They shared their food gladly and generously; they praised God and were looked up to by everyone."

Help us, Jesus, to share our goods with people in need of them and our faith with people in need of light and peace. And, always, let us be joy-filled to overflowing as we praise you, saving friend.

Bless us as we try to create community.

1 Corinthians 1:10 _____

Let us pray for unity among ourselves. As Saint Paul says, "I urge you, in the name of our Lord Jesus Christ, not to have factions among yourselves but all to be in agreement in what you profess; so that you are perfectly united in your beliefs and judgements."

Merciful God, prompt us to put aside our differences peacefully. Through free and honest discussion may we work out our problems and be united.

Only in this way can we create the community to which we are called by your Son, Jesus.

1 Corinthians 12:27 _____

We are the Body of Christ. As Paul told the Corinthians, "Now Christ's body is yourselves, each of you with a part to play in the whole."

Jesus, this is a startling way of telling us that we do have a role in the good of the Church and the world. Frequently, it's difficult to claim that we do have a part to play in the larger picture. It's easy to feel insignificant, even useless. We need this reminder that by playing our part in creating community, adding a little love to the world, and acting justly, we do build your family, your Body.

Help us to act our part worthily.

1 Corinthians 3:3 _____

Paul reminded the Corinthians about blocks to building community, "As long as there are jealousy and rivalry among you, that surely means that you are still living by your natural inclinations and by merely human principles."

If we profess to be Christians, may we put aside jealousy and rivalry. Strife fills the world. We pray that among us it will cease.

God, help us to realize the divisiveness of envy and foolish competitiveness. Give us generous and cooperative spirits.

1 Corinthians 12:4–7 _____

Saint Paul tells us: "There are many different gifts, but it is always the same Spirit; there are many different ways of serving, but it is always the same Lord. . . . The particular manifestation of the Spirit granted to each one is to be used for the general good."

God, you have gifted each one of us with unique potential to do good for the human family. Let us take a moment to thank God in silence for our talents and skills. [Pause.]

Gracious God, we thank you for these gifts, unique to each one of us. Let us never be jealous of talents we don't have, but rather let us rejoice in who you have made us and dedicate our gifts to the general good.

Galatians 5:13–15 _____

What Paul told the Galatians applies to us as well. He said, "Be servants to one another in love, since the whole of the Law is summarised in the one commandment: You must love your neighbour as yourself. If you go snapping at one another and tearing one another to pieces, take care: you will be eaten up by one another."

God, we have all seen the destruction to relationships when people tear into one another. Sometimes the snapping is behind people's backs, sometimes face-to-face. Either way, it crushes and divides.

Guide us, gracious God, to treat others with the same care that we want for ourselves.

Ephesians 4:15–16 _____

Paul tells the Ephesians and us: "If we live by the truth and in love, we shall grow completely into Christ, who is the head by whom the whole Body is fitted and joined together, every joint adding its own strength, for each individual part to work according to its function. So the body grows until it has built itself up in love."

We want to build up our community, the Body of Christ, but we sometimes feel insignificant or unnoticed and want to give up trying.

Jesus, send your Spirit to inflame our search for truth and love. Then we can become builders of your Body on earth.

Genesis 11:4 _____

When we talk together, sometimes we are like the people of Babel who stopped listening and used communication to "make a name for" themselves.

God, you want us to communicate with respect and care for one another.

Help us to have open ears and hospitable minds as we listen, share, and build community instead of disunity.

Philippians 2:1–4 _____

As we build the sense of community, let's take Paul's words to the Philippians to heart: "If in Christ there is anything that will move you, any incentive in love, any fellowship in the Spirit, any warmth or sympathy—I appeal to you, make my joy complete by being . . . one in love, one in heart and one in mind. . . . everyone pursuing not selfish interests but those of others."

Holy Spirit, in Jesus we have the example of love and fellowship to follow as we create community.

Help us to follow his example with determination and joy.

Ending

We lift our voices to our God, who gathers us together in the name of Jesus. Amen.

CHAPTER 5

Creation

Call to presence

- May we remember that the God who created us is present now.

- The God who created all things and sees them as good is with us as we pray.

- We acknowledge your presence, creator of the universe.

Prayers

Genesis 1:31

God made women and men in the divine image and likeness and saw that all that God made was good. Sky, streams, soil, and seasons all reflect the majesty of the creator.

Help us, God, to respect and protect all of your creation, remembering that you created it and gave it to us for our home. Creation is good.

May we remember that fact today and pay our homage to the earth by our actions.

Genesis 2:15

The God of all creation settled humankind on the earth. In the Scriptures, God tells us to "cultivate and take care of it."

But we have not taken very good care of it. We have polluted and trashed it, sent acid rain to burn up the trees, bulldozed the rain forests, and poured pesticides in streams.

Give us a new attitude of care and concern for your creation. Help us recall your command to take care of your handiwork—all the earth and its inhabitants.

Romans 12:4–5   _____

We celebrate our unique creation, our individual gifts. Saint Paul says, "Just as each of us has various parts in one body, and the parts do not all have the same function: in the same way, all of us, though there are so many of us, make up one body in Christ, and as different parts we are all joined to one another."

Creator God, you have made us in different sizes and shapes, as men and women, in various colors, with vastly different skills and talents.

Form all of us with all our differences into one family, each of us wonderfully unique but all of us united in charity.

1 Corinthians 3:16–17   _____

The words of Saint Paul reveal how wonderful we have been made by our creator God. He says that we are temples "of God with the Spirit of God living in" us. "God's temple is holy;" and we "are that temple."

These words show our true beauty in God's eyes, even if we sometimes cannot see the beauty in ourselves.

Creator, give us eyes to see the holy temple that you made when you created us. Send us the grace to take care of our temple, so that it is a fit dwelling place for the Spirit of truth and life.

Ending

This prayer we offer to you, God of all creation. Amen.

CHAPTER 6

Faith

Call to presence

- With faith, we pray now to you, God, present with us.

- As a believing people, we gather in prayer before our faithful God.

- In faith, let us recall the presence of God.

Prayers

Mark 1:15

John the Baptist told everyone he saw that "'the time is fulfilled, and the kingdom of God is close at hand. Repent, and believe the gospel.'"

These words were proclaimed two thousand years ago, but still most of us need to repent and believe in the Good News that Jesus brought. Jesus, you came to tell us that God loves us. You came to remind us that the Kingdom of God is created when we love our brothers and sisters as we love ourselves. You called us to love God. We want to repent and to believe.

Strengthen our weak faith, and give us courage to love as you taught us to.

Mark 6:50 _____

Jesus said many times to different people, "Do not be afraid; only have faith."

But faith is not always easy to have, especially when we are afraid. A lot of fear is going around: fear of not being accepted, fear of poverty, fear of other people's anger or spite.

Jesus, give us faith that you made us good people, that we can love and learn and lead lives with meaning and hope as you intended us to. Grant us faith that you are with us because, in our fear, we are not always sure.

James 2:26 _____

James reminds us that our faith and love are only talk unless we show them in deeds of justice, service, love, and kindness. He says, "As a body without a spirit is dead, so is faith without deeds."

Talk is cheap, but actions have value. Caring for others, behaving justly, and treating others with concern and appreciation requires strength, wisdom, and insight—all of which come with God's help.

So once again, faithful God, we ask for what we need. Help us act on our convictions. Help us get beyond hopeful talk to actual deeds done out of love.

John 6:35 _____

Jesus, you say:

> I am the bread of life.
> No one who comes to me will ever hunger;
> no one who believes in me will ever thirst.

We are hungry for your bread and thirsty for your living waters. But sometimes our lack of faith is like a person with a cold who passes a bakery and cannot smell the fragrance of baking bread. In proportion to our faith, our heart and mind are opened to you, and we are fed and nourished.

May our faith grow, Jesus our friend, so that nourished by your bread and living waters, we may nourish others. Open our heart to firm belief.

John 14:12

Jesus says,

> "Whoever believes in me
> will perform the same works as I do myself,
> and will perform even greater works."

Our faith in you gives us power to do great good for our neighbors. You healed the sick, raised the dead, and gave sight to the blind. It's hard to imagine us doing even greater works, but we have your promise that we can if we believe enough. Great faith leads to great works; weak faith leads to weak works.

Jesus, increase our faith, so that we can perform the same works as you did.

Mark 1:12–13

No one is free of temptations. Even Jesus was tempted. Mark's Gospel says, "The Spirit drove him into the desert and he remained there for forty days, and was put to the test by Satan."

 Because Jesus was tempted, we are in good company when we are tempted to do wrong. And just as God looked after Jesus, God cares for us too.

May we have the faith to ask for God's help when things are going badly and when we are tempted to be less than we can be. With God's love for us, all the tests will only strengthen our faith and hope.

Matthew 5:3

Jesus taught us that "blessed are the poor in spirit: / the kingdom of Heaven is theirs."

Let us be poor in spirit; that is, let us realize that everything comes from God for the good of all humankind. May we live simply, not be possessed by our possessions, and share generously with those of our brothers and sisters who are in need, knowing full well that our faithful God will protect and guide us.

God, give us an increase in faith, so that we may rest in you, the only true source of rest.

Matthew 13:57 _____

When Jesus visited his hometown, the people rejected him. He concluded, "'A prophet is despised only in his own country and in his own house.'"

Jesus did not work many miracles there because of the people's lack of faith. Sometimes we expect the miracles in our life to be so dramatic that no one can miss them. There are many small miracles in God's creation, but without an alert faith we can overlook them.

Jesus, renew our faith in the possibilities of miracles, and help us see the miracles that happen every day in your creation.

Matthew 21:22 _____

Jesus, you told us that "'if you have faith, everything you ask for in prayer, you will receive.'"

This is both a challenge and an affirmation for us. It challenges us to grow in faith and to turn to you in prayer. It affirms our belief in your love for us.

Grant us the grace to grow in faith, so that we can move mountains—the mountains of our fears, our selfishness, our hesitancy, or our boredom in life. You always answer our prayers and give us what is best for us, even when at first glance what we receive may not seem to be what we asked for. Faith, send faith, Brother Jesus.

Romans 1:17 _____

Saint Paul told the Romans: In the Gospels "is revealed the saving justice of God: a justice based on faith and addressed to faith. As it says in scriptures: Anyone who is upright through faith will live."

Jesus, your words are truth and life to us. They tell us how to live justly and with love in our heart.

Grant us the grace to thirst for this truth, to study your words, and to live in their spirit. With the strength of faith, fed by your word, we will have full life.

Romans 10:12–13 _____

Your generosity, saving God, never ceases to amaze us. Jesus came to save us all, "The same Lord is the Lord of all, and his generosity is offered to all who appeal to him, for all who call on the name of the Lord will be saved."

We call on your name now. Save us. Start by strengthening our faith in you and our trust that your Spirit dwells within us to light our way to you. We wish to believe, so we call on your name.

Save us, God of wisdom and power.

John 1:43,46 _____

Jesus called his first disciples, not with fancy promises or rewards, but by simply saying, "Follow me."

He calls us too, and the invitation is said just as gently because friends are invited always in a kindly way. Jesus does not want slaves as companions. He wants us to freely accept his love. And he invites us over and over again. When we turn our back on him, he runs in front of us, inviting us again. When we act destructively, Jesus beckons for us to come and see his way of faith, hope, and love.

Jesus, grace us with the faith we need to follow you.

Ending

As people seeking to grow in faith, we offer this prayer in Jesus' name. Amen.

CHAPTER 7

Freedom

Call to presence

- The God who sets us free dwells with us now as we pray.

- Let us remember that the God who saves us is present here.

- God, you break the chains of sin and shame; be with us as we pray.

Prayers

Romans 3:23–24

The sacrifice of Jesus has set us free from the bonds of death and sin. Saint Paul tells us that "no distinction is made: all have sinned and lack God's glory, and all are justified by the free gift of [God's] grace through being set free in Christ Jesus."

Jesus, most amazing is God's free gift that in turn sets us free to love.

Jesus, may we use our freedom to do more than just avoid sin. May we create your peaceable reign here on earth.

Romans 12:16

Seeking wealth and social prestige is a type of slavery. In the Gospels, Jesus urges us to "pay no regard to social standing, but meet humble people on their own terms."

Jesus, after all, was poor and virtually homeless. If we want to meet him today, we must be free to see him in poor and homeless people.

Jesus, brother and friend, open our eyes so that we meet you in all our sisters and brothers.

Romans 6:22–23 _____

True freedom is freedom from sin, from all the chains that bind us, all the hate and lust, greed and jealousy, pride and inhumanity of which we are capable. Paul reminds us of this when he says, "You are set free from sin and bound to the service of God, your gain will be sanctification and the end will be eternal life. For the wage paid by sin is death; the gift freely given by God is eternal life in Christ Jesus our Lord."

You give us freedom, holy God, through Jesus, your Son. May we accept the gift by serving you.

1 Peter 2:16 _____

Jesus wants us to be free people. As the Apostle Peter tells us, "You are slaves of no one except God, so behave like free people, and never use your freedom as a cover for wickedness."

Jesus, you know that to truly love we must give love freely. True believers are free to believe or not. To live as Jesus wishes, we should not be slaves of greed, selfishness, ignorance, and desire.

Once again, we turn to God and request the wisdom and courage to overcome any slavery to wickedness that keeps us from living freely.

Galatians 5:1 _____

Saint Paul says: "Christ set us free, so that we should remain free. Stand firm, then, and do not let yourselves be fastened again to the yoke of slavery."

Jesus, you freed us from the slavery of sin. You taught us how to overcome our tendency to be greedy, selfish, and stupid. You showed us by your example how charity and justice are the acts of free people. You set us free.

Stop us when we start to put the chains back on our wrists and legs, when we are tempted to lie, cheat, and act faithlessly. Help us to stand firm and free in your path.

2 Corinthians 5:11 _____

We can talk to the all-wise and knowing God with complete freedom. As Paul says, "God sees us for what we are, and I hope your consciences do too."

When our conscience aches with the mess that we have made of things, we don't exactly want to talk about our mistakes with anyone else. We want to hide our problems and the evil of which we are capable. God, you know us for who we are. You see deep into our heart and mind. You know every inch of us. So we are free to share all that is in us, the good, the bad, and the ugly.

We hope that in our conversation, you will heal our sore conscience and strengthen our resolve to continually reform our life. Thank you, God, for letting us be free with you.

Acts 2:4 _____

Luke tells that when Pentecost day came, "[the disciples] were all filled with the Holy Spirit and began to speak different languages as the Spirit gave them power to express themselves."

Holy Spirit, we invite you into our heart and mind. Free us from our ignorance and powerlessness.

Like the disciples, may we have the power to express the love you gave us and the truth you shared. Free us from our reluctance to be your fervent followers and true believers. Holy Spirit, come to us. Come, Holy Spirit.

Ending

Jesus, the true source of liberation, hear this prayer. Amen.

CHAPTER 8

Manifestations of God's Great Love for Us

Call to presence

- The loving God is present now with us as we pray.

- May we rest in your presence, ever-loving God.

- Let us remember that the God who loves us is with us now.

Prayers

Matthew 10:29–31

Lonely, discouraged, frustrated, or angry, we sometimes feel that nobody cares—really cares—about us. Jesus reassures us through his many talks with the Apostles. He told them, "'Can you not buy two sparrows for a penny? And yet not one falls to the ground without [God] knowing. Why, every hair on your head has been counted. So there is no need to be afraid; you are worth more than many sparrows.'"

God, part of us wants to hold fast to the knowledge of your ever-present love and care for us. Another part cannot imagine you caring that much or even knowing that we exist.

God, help us believe in your constant protection and powerful love for us. You do love us. Help us to know your love down to the deepest parts of ourselves.

Proverbs 11:17 _____

Proverbs advises, "Faithful love brings its own reward, / the inflexible injure their own selves."

God of tender care, you have been flexible with us and certainly faithful. You allowed your Apostles to make all sorts of mistakes, especially Peter, who denied you three times. Even so, you forgave him and gave him the faithful love and Holy Spirit to carry on your work.

May we remember your love for us, and may we be flexible enough to take people where they are and love them in their inherent goodness and rich potential.

Mark 2:17 _____

Jesus said: "'It is not the healthy who need the doctor, but the sick. I came to call not the upright, but sinners.'"

You came for sinners, so you came to heal us, to call us, because all of us have sinned at one time or another. We have all suffered the humiliation of knowing that we have done wrong in your sight and in the sight of other people. To know that you came to heal us is blessed reassurance.

Forgive our shortcomings; help us to follow your example. And just as, out of love, you have mercy on us, may we, out of love, have mercy on one another.

Mark 6:50 _____

The Scriptures often present Jesus greeting people with the words, "'Courage! It's me! Don't be afraid!'"

Today there is a lot that we can be afraid of: families that split apart, addicts who assault people to get money for drugs, drunk drivers, and so on. Sometimes we might even be afraid of ourselves—our anger, our passions, our ignorance, and our fears. Jesus, if we remember that you are indeed with us, our fears can be turned to calm. If we really believe that you love us unconditionally, we can walk with our head up, fearlessly and courageously.

Jesus, may we remember your words, "'Courage! It's me! Don't be afraid!'" You are with us now. Banish our fears.

1 Kings 19:4 _____

When the prophet Elijah despaired of his life, he said, "'I have had enough. Take my life.'" God, you showed your love by feeding Elijah and sending him on his journey. You were his loving companion. You are our loving companion, always with us.

God, fill us with the realization that you always have and always will love us. Let this knowledge fill us with courage, hope, love, and the desire for justice as we continue on our journey.

Isaiah 41:9–10 _____

In the Scriptures, God says to us,

> "I have chosen you . . .
> do not be afraid, for I am with you;
> do not be alarmed, for I am your God."

Despite your assurances, God, we don't always trust you to be with us. Lousy things happen, and we wonder where you were.

Help us to see the glimmers of your goodness in each moment. Let us be uplifted by your love. You are with us. Let us not be afraid. So may we walk boldly forth, knowing that you are at our side.

John 1:1–9 _____

Without sunlight, the earth would die. Each night we expect the dawn and welcome the sun at its rising. Jesus is the true light. John's Gospel tells us:

> In the beginning was the Word:
> the Word was with God
> and the Word was God. . . .
> The Word was the real light
> that gives light to everyone.

Jesus, we bask in your light by listening to your word. Then we can feel your sun fill our life, so that it overflows in charity for all of suffering humankind.

Thank you, God, for the light of your Word, Jesus.

Matthew 11:28 _____

When we are overburdened by worries, work, or fear, Jesus' words in the Scriptures are affirming and calming: "'Come to me, all you who labour and are overburdened, and I will give you rest.'"

Jesus, we seek the rest from stress that you promise. You are love. You love us.

Grant us the grace to believe in your love for us, so that we may love others, thus creating a world more peaceful and harmonious. Then, in the process, we will find the rest that you promise. Bless you, Jesus, for your love.

Romans 5:8 _____

Saint Paul says, "It is proof of God's own love for us, that Christ died for us while we were still sinners."

Jesus, you are the proof of God's complete care for humankind. You gave the perfect example of life lived to the full. You cured our ills, gave us sight, calmed storms, told us the truth, shared our food, drove blasphemers from sacred places, and forgave sins. But the ultimate gift you gave for us was your very life. In this act you redeemed us from sin, greed, selfishness, slander and envy, anger and degradation. God is love, and Jesus is the proof.

Strengthen our belief that we are loved.

Romans 8:38–39 _____

Paul said to the Romans: "I am certain of this: neither death nor life, nor angels, nor principalities, nothing already in existence and nothing still to come, nor any power, nor the heights nor the depths, nor any created thing whatever, will be able to come between us and the love of God, known to us in Christ Jesus our Lord."

Loving God, you constantly remind us of your love for us. Even if we turn our back on you, you are there, sheltering, giving life, waiting for us to turn around and realize that we are loved everlastingly.

May we face your love and embrace it.

John 5:19 _____

Jesus cured paralyzed people, blind people, and lepers, but took no credit for the cures. He said,

> In all truth I tell you,
> by himself the Son can do nothing;
> he can do only what he sees the Father doing:
> and whatever the Father does the Son does too.

Jesus, by curing us, you are doing what God wills. Again, Jesus, you are a sure and powerful sign of God's love for us.

Cure us of our doubt and anxiety. May the cures in the Gospels be a reminder of God's constant parental love for us.

Ending

We lift this prayer to you, loving, compassionate God. Amen.

CHAPTER 9

Hope

Call to presence

- God, our hope, is present with us as we pray.

- God of all hope, be with us as we pray.

- Let us place ourselves in the presence of God, who is the source of all hope.

Prayers

John 6:37–39

In John's Gospel, Jesus says,

> I will certainly not reject
> anyone who comes to me,
> because I have come from heaven,
> not to do my own will,
> but to do the will of him who sent me.
> Now the will of him who sent me
> is that I should lose nothing.

Jesus, we sometimes feel lost, purposeless, and confused. We feel better knowing that even if we wander, we can come to you, and you will not reject us. We welcome your reassurances that even if we are lost, you are not, and that you are with us each step of the way.

Help us to listen for your guidance. God of all hope, thank you.

Romans 15:13 _____

Hope is in short supply in our times. Much hopeless talk floats over the airwaves and fills even brief conversations. But Jesus was a person of hope, even though he was crucified unjustly.

The Apostle Paul had hope, even though he was shipwrecked, thrown in prison several times, lashed, and murdered by his enemies. Paul says, "May the God of hope fill you with all joy and peace in your faith, so that in the power of the Holy Spirit you may be rich in hope."

God of hope, grant us hope. May we trust that you are leading us ultimately to you and therefore to peace, joy, and the completion of love.

Matthew 24:44 _____

To lead an upright and charitable life according to the way of Christ requires close attention day by day. A certain alertness helps us see the movement of God in the events of our days. In the Gospels, Jesus admonishes us to "'stand ready because the Son of man is coming at an hour you do not expect.'"

Jesus, we often wait for you to make a dramatic entrance into our life, but you were born in simple surroundings to an unknown woman.

Help us to realize that you are in our midst now and that signs of your presence are everywhere. Let us be vigilant to the daily appearances of your miraculous touch. Seeing these daily miracles will give us hope.

Romans 8:18–25 _____

The Apostle Paul reminds us that glory waits those who hope in God. He says: "All that we suffer in the present time is nothing in comparison with the glory which is destined to be disclosed for us. . . . In hope, we already have salvation; in hope, not visibly present, or we should not be hoping—nobody goes on hoping for something which he [or she] can already see. But having this hope for what we cannot yet see, we are able to wait for it with persevering confidence."

Through our charity, striving for justice, and service, may we cocreate God's Reign on earth, among all people, and thus bring hope where there is despair.

John 10:10–11 _____

Jesus told his friends,

> I have come
> so that they may have life
> and have it to the full.
> I am the good shepherd:
> the good shepherd lays down his life for his sheep.

You have sacrificed for us. You have saved us, Jesus. And we are like sheep, in great need of sure direction. We make the same wrong turns time and time again. We are often led by our appetites into all sorts of dead ends, but you are here to guide us to full life. You are our hope because, as the good shepherd, you will stop us from running off a cliff and lead us to safety during the times of darkness. You are our hope.

So we thank you.

Galatians 6:9–10 _____

Paul encourages us, "Let us never slacken in doing good; for if we do not give up, we shall have our harvest in due time. So then, as long as we have the opportunity let all our actions be for the good of everybody."

In silence, let's bring to mind one way in which we can do good today. [Pause.]

Help us, Jesus, to do this good. We seek the rich harvest of your blessings.

2 Corinthians 4:13–14 _____

We pray with these words of Saint Paul: "We, too, believe and therefore we, too, speak, realising that he who raised up the Lord Jesus will raise us up with Jesus in our turn, and bring us to himself."

God, to stand in your presence and to be comforted by your love—just as Jesus was—is the source of our hope. Strengthen our belief, so that we never waver and never despair. You will raise us up with Jesus. Thank you, God, for this hope-giving reassurance.

John 14:1–3 _____

Right before the horror of his crucifixion and the glory of his Resurrection, Jesus calmed his disciples:

> Do not let your hearts be troubled. . . .
> After I have gone and prepared you a place,
> I shall return to take you to myself.

Jesus, when we hear this, hope fills us. Most of the time we are troubled by threats of war, unpaid bills, sickness in the family, deadlines, or a whole range of other things. Your promise of a place with you reassures us. We still have to deal with what's going on now. Problems don't just go away, but you give us hope. Hope lights our way through the darkness.

May we remember your words, "Do not let your hearts be troubled."

1 Thessalonians 4:13–14 _____

For all those who have died, we ask God's peace, having Paul's words as our consolation: "Be quite certain . . . about those who have fallen asleep, to make sure that you do not grieve for them, as others do who have no hope. We believe that Jesus died and rose again, and that in the same way God will bring with . . . those who have fallen asleep in Jesus."

God of hope and consolation, may all the dead be found in your embrace and rest in your peace.

Ending

We offer this prayer, firm in the hope that Jesus brings. Amen.

CHAPTER 10

Leaders

Call to presence

- Shepherd of our soul, be with us now as we pray.

- The God who empowers dwells within us.

- Let us remember that in our midst lives the Holy Spirit of God.

Prayers

Proverbs 11:14

Proverbs says: "For want of leadership a people perishes, / safety lies in many advisers."

Today, God our guide, may we appreciate and encourage our leaders, as well as the leadership potential that we have in ourselves. We need good leaders.

May we recognize those who lead us and nurture the leadership potential in ourselves.

For the good of all of us, grant us wisdom and compassion.

1 Thessalonians 5:12

Leaders, teachers, all those who guide us, need God's help and our consideration too. As Saint Paul says, "Be considerate to those who work so hard among you as your leaders in the Lord."

Let us remember all leaders but especially those who guide the church and our schools, and those government officials who strive to lead us toward a more just, peaceful, and caring society.

May God strengthen them, lead them, and give them wisdom and understanding as they work for our good and the good of all humankind.

Matthew 9:37

Leaders and those who minister to us are all too scarce. Jesus tells us, "'The harvest is rich but the labourers are few, so ask the Lord of the harvest to send out labourers to his harvest.'"

So we ask you now, most gracious God, for peaceful leaders and ministers.

By ourselves, we don't always have the strength, dynamism, and insight to take the lead in building your Reign among humankind. We rely on you, our God, to send the laborers into your harvest.

Matthew 20:26–28

Jesus must have surprised a lot of people when he said, "'Anyone who wants to become great among you must be your servant . . . just as the Son of man came not to be served but to serve.'"

True leaders are servants, but people in positions of authority don't always remember this.

Remind them, God, that they should first and foremost be enablers or supporters of those who follow. Your Son, Jesus, shared in your divinity but came among us to serve. May we and our leaders daily remember his example.

Ending

This prayer we offer in the name of Jesus, the perfect guide and leader. Amen.

CHAPTER 11

Love

Call to presence

- God, who is love, is with us now as we pray.

- God, you are the spark of love that fires inside us now.

- Let us call to mind that the God of love is present.

Prayers

John 13:34–35

Jesus said:

> I give you a new commandment:
> love one another. . . .
> It is by your love for one another,
> that everyone will recognise you
> as my disciples.

Jesus, we wish to be known as Christians. We call ourselves by that name. But do we love one another as you would wish us to? Probably not as well as you would like. Once again, we ask for your grace and divine aid, so that we can love one another. If you had told us to hate one another or to look out for number one, your teaching would be easier to follow, but our life would be filled with fear.

Thank you for telling us to love. Now, please help us to love.

Adapted from Proverbs 11:12 _____

Proverbs states, Whoever looks down on a neighbor lacks good sense; / intelligent people hold their tongue.

God of love and justice, you remind us once again to love each other with mutual respect, with the dignity that should exist among equals. We hate to be looked down upon; help us to treat others as we wish to be treated.

So assist us in holding back from cutting words, half-truths, and unfair gossip. Instead, let us love one another with kindness and in hope.

1 John 4:16 _____

"God is love, / and whoever remains in love remains in God."
Saint John tells us that the Christian life is contained in these words.

Jesus, teach us how to love. If we love other people, nature, and ourselves, we love you. Loving is not often easy; so grant us the strength, understanding, and faith to love.

1 John 3:14 _____

The Apostle John says, "We are well aware that we have passed over from death to life / because we love our brothers [and sisters]."

God, love is life-giving; hate kills. Grant us the grace to care for, listen to, empathize with, and serve one another. In loving we will have full life—a life that is joyful, hopeful, creative, and free from despair and anger. This is not an easy way of life, but it is a blessed one.

Thank you, God, for strengthening our ability to love.

1 Corinthians 13:1 _____

Love, this is the key to Christian life and human life. Saint Paul says, "Though I command languages both human and angelic—if I speak without love, I am no more than a gong booming or a cymbal clashing."

But love is the language that all of us wish to hear. Words of kindness, support, affirmation, and even challenge draw us forth to be our better selves.

May we speak with love in our heart and in our words, so that we build up rather than tear down.

Philemon 1:7 _____

Paul wrote his friend Philemon, "I have received much joy and encouragement by your love; you have set the hearts of God's holy people at rest."

Love does bring us joy and encouragement. And when love exists between people, everyone can be at rest because love excludes jealousy, mean gossip, angry disputes, coveting, and violence.

Loving God, once more remind us to love one another. All of us want to be joyful, affirmed, and at peace; love is the way. And you, God, are the source and model of love.

Matthew 22:37 _____

Matthew's Gospel tells us that the greatest commandment is to love God "'with all your heart, with all your soul, and with all your mind.'"

In other words, we are called to love God with our whole person. You, God, gave us everything we have with which to love you.

May we return it to you as worship by loving our neighbors as ourselves. We see you, our God, reflected in the images of creation, especially in the people around us. We worship you, creator, and pledge our love.

Romans 13:8 _____

Saint Paul says, "The only thing you should owe to anyone is love for one another, for to love the other person is to fulfill the law."

These words sound simple at first, but after a second hearing they present a challenge that calls for every virtue. Loving requires generosity of spirit, self-discipline, a calm heart, and a large vision of God's desire that we love everyone, even our enemies.

God of love, we once again turn to you, asking for your guidance and grace. Help us to acquire large-heartedness, clarity of purpose, purity of heart, and an ability to see through your eyes, so that we might truly love our sisters and brothers.

Romans 13:8 _____

In his letter to the Romans, Saint Paul told them, "The only thing you should owe to anyone is love for one another, for to love the other person is to fulfill the law."

Loving is the only thing we owe each other. It sounds easy, but we know that loving other people takes much courage, faith, and hope. These virtues come from God.

God, give us courage to get to know other people, to build trust with them, to hope that a caring relationship will grow. Thank you, our God, for giving us a law that tells us to love, and thank you for Jesus, who showed us how to love.

Romans 15:7 _____

Paul told the Romans, "Accept one another, then, for the sake of God's glory, as Christ accepted you."

Accepting one another is not all that simple. Some people have disturbing habits, bad manners, hot tempers, a thousand complaints about everything, sharp tongues, selfish streaks, and a host of other habits that are hard to accept. The only possible way for us to accept one another is to remember that God accepts us just as we are, hoping that we will love others in return.

Help us, loving God, to accept one another and to accept our own faults, too, because none of us is faultless.

1 Corinthians 13:2 _____

Jesus made love the center of Christian life. As Paul says, "Though I have the power of prophecy, to penetrate all mysteries and knowledge . . . if I am without love, I am nothing."

Without love, we are nothing. This is strong language—nothing. But we know that love makes us somebody special, and when we give love we feel the power of God flowing through us.

God, give us the power to love. Help us make love the center of our life and the focus of our energies. In this way, we create a wonderful life for ourselves and other people too.

1 Corinthians 13:4–7 _____

Saint Paul explains that "love is always patient and kind; love is never jealous; love is not boastful or conceited, it is never rude and never seeks its own advantage, it does not take offence or store up grievances. Love . . . finds its joy in the truth. It is always ready to make allowances, to trust, to hope and to endure whatever comes."

Love is a tall order. Maybe that is the reason so few of us love well and why we need God's grace.

God of love, help us learn to love in the ways the Apostle Paul describes. Grant us patience, kindness, generosity, humility, courtesy, honesty, hope, and courage.

Ending

God of love, we thank you for hearing our prayer. Amen. Alleluia!

CHAPTER 12

Peace and Reconciliation

Call to presence

- Let us remember that the Prince of Peace dwells among us at this moment.
- God is a peace-filled presence in our midst.
- Forgiving God, be with us now.

Prayers

Matthew 5:9

We are called to be peacemakers. In Matthew's Gospel, Jesus says, "Blessed are the peacemakers: / they shall be recognised as children of God."

Jesus tried to make peace with all people through the love he showed them. He was crucified. Gandhi and Martin Luther King, Jr., led nonviolent revolutions. They were shot. Peacemaking is no easy task, but it is sorely needed in our world today. Nations wage war with one another, and so do people. Sometimes the whole world seems loud with the sounds of shooting, if not by gunfire then at least by words that pierce and deeds that crush.

God of peace, make us instruments of your peace. Give us the loving hearts required to be peacemakers and thus your children.

Proverbs 10:12 _____

According to Proverbs, "Hatred provokes disputes, / but love excuses all offences."

God, you love us and forgive us. May love dwell in our heart and be manifest in our actions toward our neighbors. We wish to live in peace with each other.

Help us put hatred, anger, and jealousy aside. Instead of hatred, give us the courage to care for, respect, and love one another. Give us your spirit of forgiveness, so that we excuse each others' faults as you have excused our faults.

James 4:12 _____

For all the times that we have judged other people harshly, we ask forgiveness. The Scriptures say, "There is only one lawgiver and he is the only judge and has the power to save or to destroy. Who are you to give a verdict on your neighbour?"

Making cutting remarks and taking jabs at other people is so easy to do and so hard to resist. Judging a person by their clothes, brains, manners, skills, or looks seems to come naturally, even if we hate to be judged harshly ourselves. God, you have the power to judge; we do not. You are the only one who has the wisdom to see deep into the human soul; we do not.

For the times that we have been hard and unjust in judging others, we beg your pardon. Grant us the humility to leave judgments in your hands.

Colossians 3:13 _____

Forgiving hurts and healing our memories of these hurts is difficult, and yet living with anger is a kind of hell. Paul exhorted the Colossians: "Bear with one another; forgive each other if one of you has a complaint against another. The Lord has forgiven you; now you must do the same."

We sin against love constantly, but God forgives us each time.

Let us take a moment to forgive in our heart and mind one or two people who have hurt us. [Pause.] May we resolve to forgive these hurts in fact as well as in intention.

Matthew 5:23–24

Jesus tells us that being reconciled with one another is an essential part of Christian life. He says, "'If you are bringing your offering to the altar and there remember that your brother [or sister] has something against you, leave your offering there before the altar, go and be reconciled with your brother [or sister] first, and then come back and present your offering.'"

God, move us to seek reconciliation and peace with those whom we have offended. Give us the courage to put aside our differences, whether major or petty, so that we can live in harmony. Grant us the grace to see Jesus in all our sisters and brothers.

Matthew 7:1–2

We like to sit in judgment of other people, but God's word says, "'Do not judge, and you will not be judged; because the judgements you give are the judgements you will get.'"

This word of God scares us because some of our judgments can be tough on other people.

God, rather than judging, may our attitude be tolerant of and hopeful about other people. You forgave people who offended you, even those who betrayed you. It's easy to pass harsh judgments, but we don't like to be judged. Let us treat others as we wish to be treated ourselves.

Matthew 15:30

Our heart often needs healing. It needs to be healed of anger and jealousy, bitterness and despair. In his Gospel, Matthew tells us, "Large crowds came to [Jesus] bringing the lame, the crippled, the blind, the dumb and many others; these they put down at his feet, and he cured them."

Jesus, we want to believe that you can heal our heart and body.

Today, we pray that you will see into our heart and cure us of evil intentions, self-delusion, dishonesty, and hopelessness. Give us the heart to love our neighbors as we love ourselves. Heal our heart, merciful Jesus.

Matthew 18:22 _____

Peter once asked Jesus how often he should forgive people who did him wrong. Much to his disappointment, "Jesus answered, 'Not seven, I tell you, but seventy-seven times.'"

Jesus, this seems like a lot of abuse to take from anyone. Forgiving, even once, is not easy for us. In our world we are told not to get angry but to get even. So when you tell us to forgive seventy-seven times, please understand our problems with that. If that is your way, okay, but we will need your grace to be so forgiving.

Once again, we ask for your grace to always be ready to forgive and be reconciled. O God, come to our assistance.

Romans 2:1 _____

We do injustice to our neighbors by judging them, often before we really know them. In his letter to the Romans, Paul warns us, "It is yourself that you condemn when you judge others, since you behave in the same way as those you are condemning."

Let's look to our own conduct today. May we clean up our own act before we judge others. Since this is a project of a lifetime, we won't have time to condemn our sisters and brothers.

Instead of harsh criticisms directed at our neighbors, may we speak kindly, act justly, and live tolerantly.

Romans 12:18–21 _____

When we are hurt, insulted, embarrassed, or outwitted, we are sorely tempted to seek vengeance on those whom we target as our enemies. One evil often calls forth another evil from us. But Christians are called to something else. Paul told the Romans: "As much as is possible, and to the utmost of your ability, be at peace with everyone. Never try to get revenge. . . . Do not be mastered by evil, but master evil with good."

This is another hard teaching that goes against all those voices that goad us by saying, "Are you going to let them get away with that?"

God, make us instruments of peace and justice, not revenge and retaliation. Left to ourselves we will pay back with evil, but with your help we can be reconcilers.

Adapted from John 17:21,23 _____

God wishes us to overcome all our differences and to be united in peace. Jesus says, "May all people be one, like God and I are one. May all in the community of believers be so perfectly united that the world will say, 'God sent Jesus, and God loves the community just as God loves Jesus.'"

Settling conflicts and making peace create unity.

Jesus, may we be filled with the desire for peaceful relationships, and may we take the practical steps to be united, steps like talking to those with whom we are in conflict, forgiving those who have offended us, and asking pardon from those we have wronged. Jesus, help us to be united. Send your peace.

Acts 3:19–20 _____

In order to be reconciled with God and the community of believers, we need to follow Peter's advice: "'Now you must repent and turn to God, so that your sins may be wiped out, and so that the Lord may send the time of comfort.'"

God, we wish to be cleansed from all our wrongdoings.

Help us turn to you in honesty and in hope. With your grace we can turn our life around toward you, God of mercy. Then we will be comforted. Just in case we become too complacent, remind us that we are not perfect in this life.

2 Corinthians 5:19 _____

Saint Paul tells us that in Christ, we have been reconciled to God and that the work of reconciliation is now entrusted to us. He says, "God was in Christ reconciling the world to [God], not holding anyone's faults against them, but entrusting to us the message of reconciliation."

In one sentence, we have both good news and a heavy responsibility.

Thank you for the good news that Jesus has reconciled us. Help us now to be a people of peace and reconciliation. Help us to take up the task that we have inherited from Jesus. We can make peace and build reconciliation with your courage in our heart and your wisdom in our mind.

Colossians 3:13–15 _____

God invites us to new life in Jesus and to communion with all believers. Saint Paul says, "Bear with one another; forgive each other if one of you has a complaint against another. The Lord has forgiven you; now you must do the same. . . . Put on love, the perfect bond. And may the peace of Christ reign in your hearts. . . ."

God, we do desire the peace that comes with forgiveness.

We ask for the courage and compassion to be reconciled with one another. Help us to take the first steps by forgiving.

Ending

We offer this prayer in the name of Jesus, Prince of Peace and source of all reconciliation. Amen.

CHAPTER 13

Trust in Providence

Call to presence

- The God who provides us with life lives within us.

- God of all goodness be here with us.

- As we pray, let us rest in God.

Prayers

Philippians 4:6–7

Joy is a true sign of God's presence and blessings. It comes with our trust in God's providence. God is here. God is with us. So, as Saint Paul told the Philippians, "Never worry about anything; but tell God all your desires of every kind in prayer and petition shot through with gratitude, and the peace of God which is beyond our understanding will guard your hearts."

Instead of worrying, in a moment of silence tell God some of your desires and ask for more trust in God's providence. [Pause.]

God, you are listening to what we want. May we be open to what you want for us—joy and peace.

Matthew 6:20–21

We are often told to trust in this or that product, from cars to microwaves, deodorants to sunglasses, wood stain to siding. But Jesus says, "'Store up treasures for yourselves in heaven, where neither moth nor woodworm destroys them and thieves cannot break in and steal. For wherever your treasure is, there will your heart be too.'"

Jesus, let us keep on a track to you. Help us to avoid being owned by what we own. Instead of trusting in property or wealth, may we trust in you.

Only you give our life meaning and purpose. Thank you.

Matthew 6:25,33–34

Jesus tells us not to worry about life but to set our heart on God's "'kingdom first, and on God's saving justice. . . . Do not worry about tomorrow: tomorrow will take care of itself.'"

Jesus, we are tempted to say, "That's easy for you to say, you were not only human but also divine."

Instead, we ask you to help us overcome our defensiveness and our fear. Aid us in getting our priorities straight. May we put love of you and our neighbors first. This is the key to the joy that you promise. Trust is not easy. Jesus, help us.

Matthew 18:20

We can trust in God's providence because Jesus is always with us. We only need to acknowledge that consoling presence. Jesus assures us, "'Where two or three meet in my name, I am there among them.'"

Jesus, your words are filled with hope. As we gather in your name today, you are here to uphold and enlighten us. You are infinitely trustworthy.

Let us believe in you completely and rest in your divine presence today.

Matthew 19:23

Jesus always seemed to say things that challenge us to trust in God's providence rather than wealth or possessions. Especially strong is his statement, "It is hard for someone rich to enter the kingdom of Heaven."

But so many forces in our culture tell us to collect and to save, to buy and to consume. Jesus, we believe that your point is that we should not hoard money, or food, or talents when other people—our neighbors—are starving, or alone, or in need.

Help us trust that when we are generous you will always provide, that when we give, we will receive your blessings.

Matthew 28:20 _____

Jesus, after his Resurrection, appeared to the disciples and told them, "'I am with you always; yes, to the end of time.'"

Be with us now, Jesus. May your presence strengthen our trust that we too will be raised with you. You are all consolation and inspiration. Confident in your presence at all times, may we banish fear from our heart, seek after justice and peace, and live with enthusiasm and hope.

You are with us, always upholding us. Praise be to you, Jesus our Savior.

Philippians 4:6–7 _____

Saint Paul told his friends, "Never worry about anything; but tell God all your desires of every kind in prayer and petition shot through with gratitude, and the peace of God which is beyond our understanding will guard your hearts."

Gracious God, you want us to tell you our needs. Let's each, in a moment of silence, ask God for what we most need right now. [Pause briefly.]

And God, grant us the peace that comes from a trust in your love for us.

Galatians 5:22–23 _____

God's providence is opened to us in the gifts of the Holy Spirit. In his letter to the Galatians, Saint Paul described these gifts: "The fruit of the Spirit is love, joy, peace, patience, kindness, goodness, trustfulness, gentleness and self-control."

Holy Spirit, you invite us to share in these gifts. We trust that in calling on you, you will help us to be people of love, joy, and peace.

Holy Spirit, come into our heart, mind, and will. Fill us with your gifts.

Ending

In complete trust in your providence, we lift our voices to you, ever-faithful God. Amen.

CHAPTER 14

Wisdom and Understanding

Call to presence

- Let us remember that the all-wise God is with us as we pray.
- The God who knows and understands all things is with us.
- Come, Holy Spirit, and send your light upon us.

Prayers

John 17:25–26 _____

Jesus once prayed in this way:

> Upright One, . . .
> I have made your name known to them
> and will continue to make it known,
> so that the love with which you loved me may be in them,
> and so that I may be in them.

God of all wisdom, open our heart and mind to your name, to your mercy, so that we can finally acknowledge that all along you have loved us. May we be warmed and empowered by your love.

But first, teach us to know you through listening to your words spoken and modeled by Jesus. He is always with us to teach and guide us. Upright one, may we know your name.

James 1:5

In his epistle, James writes, "Any of you who lacks wisdom must ask God, who gives to all generously and without scolding."

Thank you, God, for these reassuring words. Grant us wisdom, because to live calmly and at peace with other people today demands a wisdom beyond what we have. To see our problems and to deal with other people justly sometimes seems like an impossible ideal.

Grant us wisdom, God, source of wisdom. And thank you for not scolding us, for not expecting us to be wiser than we are, and for reminding us that wisdom is given by you if we but ask.

Titus 2:11

We are sometimes tempted to think that Jesus came to save only us. We can become self-righteous about our religion, our faith, and our salvation. But the Apostle Paul declares, "You see, God's grace has been revealed to save the whole human race."

Jesus revealed God to humankind, so that all of us could be brought to freedom, love, hope, and perfect faith. We are not the only ones who have heard God's call.

Saving God, help us to hear your word spoken by other believers; may we learn from them and work with them to build up your people.

Mark 3:35

Jesus is always trying to make things clear for us. And so he says, "'Anyone who does the will of God, that person is my brother and sister.'"

The will of God is contained in the two great commandments to love God and our neighbors. By love we become not only sisters and brothers of Jesus but sisters and brothers to all people.

Gracious God, help us to learn from Jesus how to love and, therefore, how to do your will. By being brothers and sisters to all humankind, we build the world family. For your guidance, we pray.

Ecclesiasticus 37:16

In Ecclesiasticus, God warns us, "Reason should be the basis for every activity, / reflection must come before any undertaking."

Holy Spirit, as we gather here, inform our reasons, enlighten our reflection. With you, Holy Spirit, our work will come to good, our efforts will lead to justice. Let us not be moved by ungovernable passions and hasty judgments. Spirit of wisdom, grant us your wisdom and understanding.

Mark 3:35

Jesus tells us that "'anyone who does the will of God, that person is my brother and sister.'"

Jesus, in particular circumstances, knowing God's will is not so simple.

Even so, help us to know it. May we read the Scriptures and be open to your words there. Also, help us to hear God's will in the cries of poor and helpless people and by listening to one another. We wish to be your brothers and sisters.

Adapted from Ephesians 1:17–19

As Paul prayed with the Ephesians, so let us pray: May the God of Jesus our Savior give us wisdom and understanding of all that has been revealed. May we marvel at God's work and see the hope that God offers us. The inheritance God grants to us is rich. Great is the power of our God. Amen.

Matthew 5:6

Jesus tells us that "blessed are those who hunger and thirst for uprightness: / they shall have their fill."

God, we do hunger and thirst for dignity and integrity, but it's often easy to despair that we will ever stick to the way of truth and light.

All-wise God, fill us with wisdom, understanding, and the willpower that we need to be upright sisters and brothers, your beloved children. Guide us, all-wise God. Lead us, kindly light.

Matthew 7:15–16

How can we know the truth? We are given half-truths and un-truths all the time. People are always trying to sell us a bill of goods. Promises tempt us in all directions. Jesus offers us a guide when he says, "'Beware of false prophets. . . . You will be able to tell them by their fruits.'"

Jesus, may we have the sense to follow your advice and look at the results of all the promises made to us.

May we have the wisdom to recognize genuine promises in good fruit: care, justice, and peace. Help us to recognize false promises and fake prophets in the rotten fruit of careless-ness, injustice, and warfare.

Matthew 13:31–32

God's Reign is "'like a mustard seed which a man took and sowed in his field. It is the smallest of all seeds, but when it has grown it is the biggest of shrubs and becomes a tree, so that the birds of the air can come and shelter in its branches.'"

Jesus, may we be like the earth that welcomes the mus-tard seed.

May we nourish your word in our soul, so that as your way grows in us, we may have the rich generosity of the tree that gives itself for the good of others.

John 8:31–32

We have this promise from Jesus:

> If you make my word your home
> you will indeed be my disciples;
> you will come to know the truth,
> and the truth will set you free.

Jesus, we do want the truth that will set us free, free from our compulsions, free from our loneliness and sadness, free from anger and divisions.

May your words become a home for us. As we study your word, we will encounter your truth, the truth that you love us and have saved us. Then we will be free. Open our eyes, ears, heart, and mind.

Romans 12:2 _____

Saint Paul warned his people to be wary of the values of the world. He said, "Do not model your behaviour on the contemporary world, but let the renewing of your minds transform you, so that you may discern for yourselves what is the will of God—what is good and acceptable and mature."

We too are challenged to renew our mind by prayer, by listening to the word of God, and by following the law of loving our neighbors as ourselves.

God, renew and transform us. We want to do your will. Show us what it is, so that we can do good and grow in your image.

John 7:24 _____

Jesus says, "'Do not keep judging according to appearances; let your judgement be according to what is right.'"

We are frequently tempted to judge people based on how they dress, on their fatness or thinness, or on other idiosyncrasies. By doing this, we don't need to be bothered with who they really are. We refuse to become involved in searching for the heart of the matter or for what is right. True wisdom seeks to know the whole story.

God, send your Spirit into our heart and mind so that we find out the truth and judge accordingly. Make us seekers after truth.

1 Corinthians 1:25–28 _____

The Apostle Paul says: "God's folly is wiser than human wisdom, and God's weakness is stronger than human strength. . . . God chose those who by human standards are . . . weak to shame the strong . . . so that no human being might feel boastful before God."

God, we are often weak. So we must depend on you. You are the source of true wisdom and strength, and these are contained in your word made flesh, Jesus the Christ.

Help us to count on your wisdom and strength to make up for our ignorance and weakness.

1 Corinthians 2:10–12 _____

In Paul's letter to the Corinthians, he said, "God has given rev-
elation through the Spirit, for the Spirit explores the depths of
everything, even the depths of God. . . . The Spirit we have
received is . . . God's own Spirit, so that we may understand
the lavish gifts God has given us."

Let us take a moment of silence to value one or two of the
talents, skills, or gifts that God has given us. [Pause.]

For all these gifts, given out of your love, we thank you,
God of all goodness.

Adapted from Ephesians 3:14–21 _____

Let's share in this prayer that Paul said for the Ephesians: I
pray, kneeling before God. In the abundance of God's glory
may God—through the Holy Spirit—enable us to grow firm
in power with regard to our inner self. May Christ live in our
heart through faith. And then, rooted in love, with all the people of God we will have the power to comprehend the depth
of reality. Wrapped in Christ's love, we are filled with the fullness of God.

Glory be to our God whose power surpasses anything we
can imagine. This power works in us. All praise be to you,
God, forever and ever in Jesus. Amen.

Matthew 20:34 _____

Matthew tells us that when the blind men asked Jesus for
sight, he "felt pity for them and touched their eyes, and at
once their sight returned and they followed him."

Jesus, give us new sight. Help us see the wonders of your
world, the talents you have given us, the beauty of goodness.
Grant us the wisdom and understanding that comes from the
sight you give.

Yours is true sight that will save the world.

Adapted from Ephesians 5:15–17 _____

In his letter to the Ephesians, Saint Paul reminded himself and
his people to be very careful about the sort of lives we lead.
May we be insightful, not senseless people, so that we can

make the best of the present time. It is a wicked age. We want to recognize your will.

Our present world too often feeds us a line contrary to what Jesus spoke and modeled.

Spirit of God, give us the good sense to take Jesus' words and example to heart and make them our own.

Ending

This prayer we offer to you, Spirit of wisdom and understanding. Amen.